W9-CFJ-910

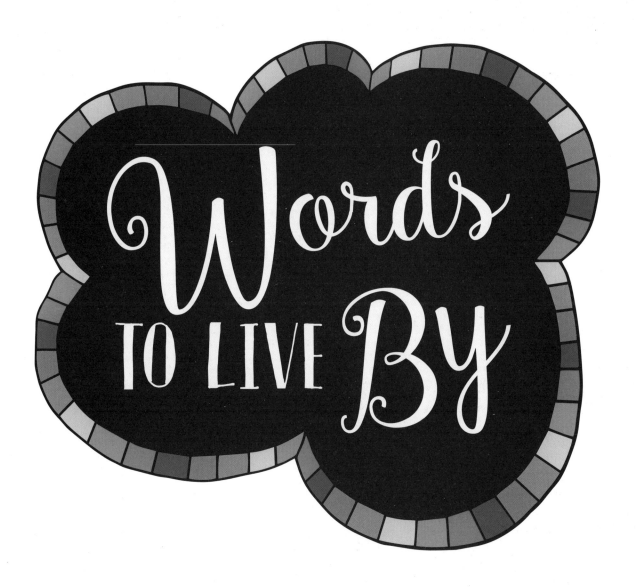

Words TO LIVE By

by Dawn Nicole Warnaar

INTRODUCTION

If you're holding this book, it's probably safe to assume that you have an interest in lettering and art. Whether you're a pro or a "newbie," it can be easy to compare your work to others. I want to encourage you not to do that and remind you that the expert in anything was once a beginner. What I love so much about art is that anything goes! Developing your own unique style comes with time and practice. Create, draw, letter, and doodle just for the sake of simply creating. Try to create something every day, even if it's small. You will be amazed by how your skills grow just by simply practicing your art form. Keep all your sketch pads. Look back at your work from time to time. You will realize how far you've come, and you might even be surprised to see that you have already found your personal style. Just create. And have fun doing it!

GET Lost in RIGHT the DIRECTION

Art enables us to find ourselves & lose ourselves at the same time.
-Thomas Morton

HAVE FUN!

LETTERING TOOLS

There are so many different kinds of lettering tools out there, but it can get overwhelming having so much to choose from. I'm going to focus on the basics you need to get started, because one of my favorite things about hand-lettering is that you don't really need fancy tools! Below are the basic supplies I use for almost every lettering project I do.

Sketch Pad: I'm partial to the 11" x 14" size with paper that has a medium surface (made for dry media, like sketching) and a 70 lb. weight that is thick enough to stand up to markers.

Straightedge/Ruler: I'm partial to clear rulers because you can see through them while you're working. In addition to a basic straightedge, I use a T-square style ruler almost every time I letter a project. It makes it extra easy to draw nice straight lines on the page.

Pencils: Any pencils will do. Just make sure they're nice and sharp. I prefer non-mechanical pencils. If you're feeling fancy, try Palomino® Blackwing pencils. I use them for all my lettering and drawing.

Erasers: If you're like me, you'll go through the erasers on your pencils fast, so it's really handy to have a larger eraser nearby, especially if you're tackling a large area. My favorite erasers are Papermate® Black Pearl erasers.

Markers: After I sketch in pencil, I go back and outline with black markers. I like to keep an assortment of marker styles on hand; but at minimum, I always have a fine and ultra-fine permanent marker nearby.

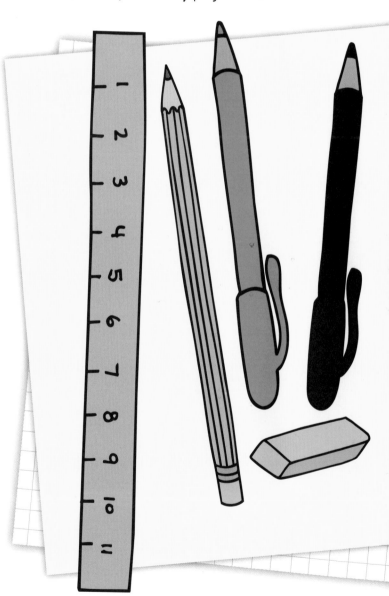

LETTERING BASICS

Serif Fonts:

If you pick up a book in your home and look at the text inside, you'll most likely find what is called a serif font. Serif fonts have little lines or curves at the ends of the letter strokes.

Sans Serif Fonts:

Sans means "without." Sans serif fonts are "without" serif. They are very basic fonts and do not have any little lines or curves at the ends of the letter strokes.

Script Fonts:

Script fonts, also known as cursive fonts, are what I call the "fancy fonts." Calligraphy is a type of script font. The letters are often (but not always) connected in this type of font.

ANATOMY OF A LETTER

Did you know letters have parts? They do! In fact, they have quite a few. This is not a comprehensive list of all the parts, but it's a great foundation to get started learning about the anatomy of letters.

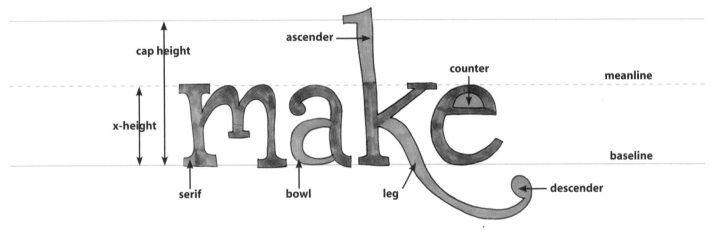

Baseline: The invisible line where all characters sit.

Meanline: The imaginary line running along the top of non-ascending, lowercase letters.

Cap Height: The height of capital letters from the baseline to the top of the capital letter.

X-Height: The height of the body of a lowercase letter.

Ascender: A vertical stroke found on lowercase letters that extends above the letter's x-height. Letter examples with ascenders include *b, d, f, h, k,* and *l*.

Descender: A vertical stroke found on lowercase letters that extends below the baseline. Letter examples with descenders include *g, j, p, q,* and *y*. Due to the way I've drawn it here, my letter *k* has a descender. Because it is decorative, it may also be referred to as a **tail** or **swash**.

Serif: The foot or feet found on a serif style letter.

Counter: The space (full or partial) within a letter.

Bowl: The curved stroke that goes around a letter's counter. Letter examples with **counters** and **bowls** include: *B/b, D/d, O/o, P/p,* and *Q/q*.

Arm/Leg: A horizontal or vertical stroke that is attached only on one end. Letter examples with an **arm** include *E, F, L,* and *T*. Letter examples with a **leg** include *R* and *K/k*.

Crossbar/Bar: A horizontal stroke on a letter. Examples include the letters E/*e*, F/*f*, *t*, and *A*.

FIVE TIPS FOR HAND-LETTERED DESIGN

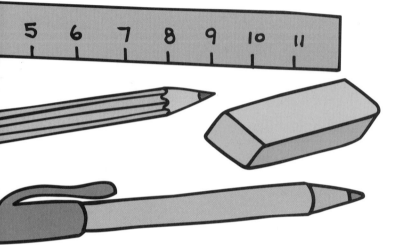

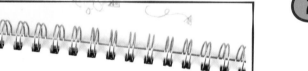

1 USE THE RIGHT TOOLS

Good writing tools are essential. You don't have to have the top of the line, but it's worth investing in a few quality pieces! For nearly every lettering project I do, I use sharpened pencils, a straightedge, and a T-square ruler, erasers, and markers.

2 SKETCH OUT YOUR IDEAS

Even most of the world's best logo designers and hand-letterers start by sketching out ideas. In my graphic design classes, we were required to sketch out at least one whole page of ideas. To this day, I still start every project this way. Some of your best ideas will come out of "brainstorming on paper."

3 SKETCH YOUR CHOSEN DESIGN IN PENCIL FIRST

Since you don't want to mess up on your final design, always sketch in pencil first so you can make sure the layout and spelling are correct. I like to use a ruler to lightly draw in guidelines to keep my text straight and evenly sized.

4 MAKE IT PERMANENT

Now is when I use my markers to start tracing lines and filling in space. Take your time to avoid mistakes and smearing (especially if you are a lefty like me). When your design is fully dry, erase any visible pencil lines.

5 ADD DETAILS

Add some details like doodles and flourishes. Try unexpected things to add an artistic touch. In this piece, I purposefully smeared my work to give it an inky look. I used a water-based brush pen to do the lettering and then gently smeared it with a barely damp piece of paper towel until I was happy with the overall look.

THE BASICS OF FONT PAIRING

When it comes to mixing fonts, you'll get differing opinions, but there are a few general rules that will have you font pairing like a pro. But like Pablo Picasso said, "Learn the rules like a pro, so you can break them like an artist."

You'll find some sources that give a long list of font-pairing rules, but I think most of them boil down to two basics:

1. OPPOSITES ATTRACT

In these examples, you can see that all of these font pairings are opposites!

2. KEEP IT SIMPLE

Using two or three fonts in one piece is plenty. If you use more than that, you'll end up with a piece that's too chaotic.

HOW TO MIX 2 FONTS

PLAIN & fancy

THICK + THIN

serif and sans serif

ALL CAPS + lowercase

TOUGH & Girly

SKETCH HERE

HOW TO DO FAUX CALLIGRAPHY

As beautiful as traditional calligraphy is, it takes years to perfect!
There's an easy way to get a faux-calligraphy look in just a few simple steps.

STEP ONE
Sketch out your ideas in pencil, and then sketch your chosen design onto your sketch pad.

STEP TWO
Trace the design with an ultra-fine point marker.

STEP THREE

Thicken any downstrokes. Downstrokes are the lines that occur anytime you draw downward when you create letters. I've shown you where they are by adding a double line to all of my downstrokes.

STEP FOUR

Color in the downstrokes to create thicker lines. Allow the ink to dry, and erase your pencil lines.

And that's all there is to it! Pretty neat, right?

SKETCH HERE

30-DAY LETTERING CHALLENGE

Practice your lettering by sketching one of these prompts each day for 30 days!

Your Name	Just Create	Kindness Changes Everything	You're My Favorite	Be Happy
Do What You Love	Draw All Day	Choose Joy	Live. Laugh. Love.	Shine Bright
Dream Big	Have Courage	Family	Celebrate	Oh Hey There!
Be Awesome Today	You're the Best	Daydreamer	Stop & Smell the Flowers	Adventure Awaits
Hello Sunshine	Stay Sweet	Be The Good	Chin Up Buttercup	Love Life
Rise and Shine	Oh Happy Day!	Make Your Own Luck	Work Hard & Be Nice	Good Things to Come

HELLO SUNSHINE

SKETCH HERE

have Courage

rise & shine

Do what you LOVE

Adventure awaits

30-DAY DRAWING/DOODLE CHALLENGE

Practice your doodling and drawing skills by sketching one of these subjects each day for 30 days!

Sunshine	Cupcakes	Zoo Animal	Swirls	Shooting Stars
Rainbows	Arrows	Ice Cream	Alphabet	Trees
Cherries	Ocean Waves	Umbrella	Daisies	Concentric Circles
Zigzags	Hearts	Leaves	Polka Dots	Self-Portrait
Stripes	Unicorn	Confetti	Apples	Cactus
Clouds	Snowflakes	Light Bulbs	Teardrops	Spirals

SKETCH HERE

DOODLED ALPHABET

I'm always saying "Sketch it in pencil first." Well, for this project I want you to forget that rule. The point of this exercise is to just play and have fun creating. I want you to simply doodle the alphabet. You'll be amazed at how fun doodles just seem to pop off the page when you create without a plan. For that reason, we're doing this project in all markers, from the get-go!

SUPPLIES:
- Sketch pad
- Markers

STEP ONE
Doodle the whole alphabet, focusing on giving each letter its own style.

STEP TWO
Add extra doodles to some letters to create interest.

TIP!

Buy a sketch pad that can withstand markers. My favorite sketch pad is a mixed media pad with 90 lb. weight paper that has a vellum surface. I love the bigger sketch pads, usually opting for the 9" x 12" or 11" x 14" sized spiral pads.

SKETCH HERE

DOODLE ART

One of the easiest ways to get inspired is to let your words dictate the art. You can see what I mean by that with this project. I chose to hand-letter the phrase "Stay Sweet." Then I doodled all kinds of fun, sweet things around it!

SUPPLIES:
- Sketch pad
- Pencil
- Markers

STEP ONE
Pick a phrase and sketch it on your page in pencil.

STEP TWO
Fill the surrounding space with doodles that match the text.

STEP THREE
Trace all your lettering and doodles with black marker. I used a combination of fine-point and ultra-fine-point black markers.

STAY Sweet

SKETCH HERE

Here are a few more ideas for phrases
to inspire your doodle art!

Love yourself.
(Heart doodles)

"The earth has music for those who listen."
—Shakespeare
(Music notes and symbols)

Say yes to new adventures.
(Arrow doodles)

Be Happy.
(Doodle your favorite things)

SHAPE ART

Sometimes you'll have days where you feel like creating but don't know what to create. This project is perfect for those times. Shape art is simply drawing your letters and doodles within a shape. You can use stencils or freehand your shapes.

Once you pick a shape, think about what words "match" that shape. For the heart, I chose "Love what you do." For the butterfly, I opted for "Falling is a chance to fly." Don't think too much about it. Just sketch your words to fit the shape!

SUPPLIES:
- Sketch pad
- Basic art supplies (pencil, erasers, markers, watercolors, etc.)
- Stencils (optional)
- Scissors

1

LOVE
what you
DO

falling is a
chance
to fly

STEP TWO

Add color! For my heart shape, I just used markers. For my butterfly, I used a water brush to add blue watercolors as my background. Once it was totally dry, I went over my lettering with a fine tip marker. Allow shape art to dry completely before erasing out any stray pencil marks from your sketch.

TIP!

Use this method to make art that you can use to create your own cards, decorate gift packages, make DIY notebook covers, and more!

STEP THREE
Cut out your shapes, and display on a memo board in your room!

You're a deer

LOVE
what you
DO

falling is a chance to fly

I need vitamin sea

PAINT SAMPLE BOOKMARKS

This project is so much easier than it looks thanks to the use of colorful paint samples! They are the perfect size for creating DIY bookmarks. You can find paint samples at most stores that sell paint and DIY supplies. This project would be great for hosting a craft night!

SUPPLIES:

- Paint samples
- Permanent marker
- Scissors
- Hole punch
- Embroidery thread

STEP ONE
Gather a small handful of paint samples. Trim the words off some of the longer samples.

STEP TWO
Add doodles and words, leaving room to add a hole punch at the top of each bookmark. (Some of the paint samples I found already had a little hole punched in them!)

STEP THREE

③ Hole punch the top of each bookmark. Tie on embroidery thread in different colors to create a tassel.

TIP!

Try to only touch the paint samples near the edges. The oils from your skin can make it hard for the permanent marker to "stick" to the paint samples.

THIS BOOK belongs TO:

CHLOE

NEGATIVE SPACE ART

Negative space is the space around an object. In this project, I created negative space in the area between the "LOVE" lettering and the heart. By filling this negative space with doodles and color, the "LOVE" lettering really stands out. You can re-create this piece with your own doodles or try creating an original piece of negative space art using any word or object you like!

SUPPLIES:
- Sketch pad
- Pencil
- Eraser
- Markers

STEP ONE
Sketch your design in pencil on your sketch pad.

STEP TWO

Trace the outline in black marker. This is optional, but it helps you gain a better understanding of creating a negative space piece of art. You'd get the same effect without the outline. Try it both ways to see which look you prefer.

STEP THREE

Fill the negative space with doodles until the whole area is filled.

STEP FOUR

Add color! Keep a piece of scrap paper nearby to test colors on before using them in your art. A lot of markers look much different on paper than their cap colors might lead you to believe, so this will help you make sure you get the color you really want!

SKETCH HERE

HAPPY MAIL

We live in a digital age, so sending snail mail isn't as common as it used to be, but there's something so much more personal about sending a hand-written letter or note than an email. I try to make it a priority to send all my thank you notes via snail mail. You can be sure it will brighten someone's day when they open their mailbox and find a special note from you!

You can make the letters and packages you send even more special by adding an artistic touch. All you need are some plain or colored envelopes and an assortment of pens and fine-point markers. Gel pens in white, metallic, and bright colors work really well on darker colored envelopes.

SUPPLIES:
- Envelopes
- Assorted pens & markers

There aren't really "steps" for this project, just use your imagination, draw, and doodle! I used colored envelopes and black and white pens, but you can also try doodling on plain white envelopes with colored pens.

Here are four designs to help inspire you!

TIP!

Use this method to create your own giftwrap, gift bags, or to add interest and color to packages wrapped in simple brown Kraft paper.

Note Tag Envelope
It doesn't need to be overly fancy to be cute! Just doodle a little tag and put the address inside of it.

Kate Moore
123 Sunshine St.
Anywhere USA 12345

Happy Mail Envelope
Mix up the types of lettering you use (script, serif, and sans serif) and add some simple doodles, arrows, and a "Happy Mail" announcement at the bottom.

Allie King
104 MAGNOLIA
→ APT 2B
St. Louis, MO 63133

Happy Mail!

dawn nicole
149 Rainbow Row
SC
Charleston
29414

Leaf Frame
I used the white gel pen to doodle a simple leaf frame around the address. Drawing the name in a fancy script and adding a flourish under the address gives this envelope a classy, traditional look.

QUINN DAVIS
8053 Lovely Lane
ANYWHERE USA
20147

Floral Doodle Envelope
For this one, I drew a simple frame for the address and drew swirls and florals at random to create a really lovely design. I love how the white gel pen stands out on this envelope, creating a whimsical style.

MAGAZINE ART

Playing with letters and typography doesn't always mean you have to draw. Projects like this are a great way to find inspiration and study the many ways to draw letters. I often flip through magazines and clip out images, words, and letters that inspire me. I tape them all in a notebook I call my "Creative Smashbook." When I need ideas, I just flip through it for inspiration!

For this project, I chose one of my favorite Shakespeare quotes (from the play *Hamlet*), but you can use any quote or phrase you like!

SUPPLIES:
- Black card stock
- Magazines
- Scissors
- Glue
- White gel pen (optional)

STEP ONE
Choose a quote and write it down. Flip through a stack of magazines and cut out cool letters until you have all of the ones you need to create your chosen quote.

To thine own self be true.
—Shakespeare

STEP TWO
Lay them out on your paper to make
sure you like how they look. Once you
do, glue them down. Allow to dry. Use
a gel pen to add fun doodles to your
magazine art (optional).

TIP!
Spray glue that is paper-friendly
works well for this project but white
school glue is fine too. Just use
it sparingly since magazine
paper tends to be thin.

DIY STATIONERY

If there is one thing that I can't resist buying, it's cute notecards and stationery.
I love making it just as much as I love buying it. It is so easy to create!

SUPPLIES:

- Watercolor paper
- Paper trimmer or scissors
- Paintbrush or waterbrush
- Fine-point black marker

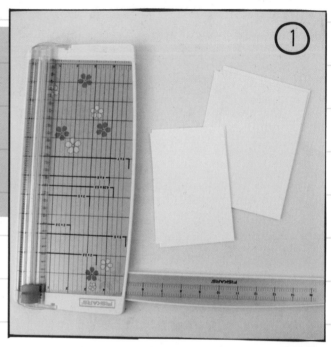

STEP ONE

Trim your watercolor paper down to stationery sizes. I made some 4" x 6" and some 5" x 7".

STEP TWO

At the top of each piece, add some simple watercolor art. I've given you some ideas you can use in the pictures! You can paint simple brushstrokes, splatters, hearts, circles, etc. Allow stationery to dry thoroughly.

TIP!

For monograms, the order of the letters is: first name initial, last name initial, middle name initial. So if your name were Sarah Jane Bailey your monogram would be SBJ. Many times, the initial of your last name will be enlarged, like you see I've done for mine, DWN, in the examples.

STEP THREE

Add your name, monogram, or text, such as "Just a note," at the top of each piece of stationery.

MAP ART

✳   I love creating things that remind me to be adventurous and get outside.
I used the phrase "Let's get lost" to remind myself to go explore without a plan. Nature and
walks can be an awesome source of inspiration for your creations!

Visit your local office supply store to find an assortment of map-patterned
scrapbook paper or use an old map you have laying around the house
(with permission if it's not yours of course!).

SUPPLIES:

- White card stock
- Map or map-patterned scrapbook paper
- Scissors
- Glue stick
- Watercolors (optional)
- Paper trimmer (optional)

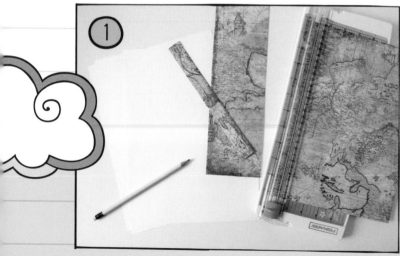

STEP ONE
Trim your map paper to
match your card stock.

(2)

STEP TWO

Use a pencil to sketch a phrase/design onto the map
paper. Depending on how dark your map is, you may
have to press down harder than usual to see your
pencil lines when you go to cut it.

STEP THREE

Carefully, cut out one letter/design at a time. Small detail scissors work well for cutting out letter centers.

TIP!

If the watercolor or glue makes your paper curl up a bit, allow it to fully dry and then place several heavy books on top of it. Allow it to sit overnight. This will "press" the map art and make it nice and flat again.

STEP FOUR

Paint your card stock with a few strokes of watercolor to add more interest to your map art. Allow it to dry completely before the next step.

STEP FIVE

Glue the map letters and designs you cut out onto your card stock. Once dry, erase any visible pencil lines on the map letters/designs. Hang and enjoy.

⑤

Let's get lost

DIY MAGNETS

I'm not normally big on clutter but I think a fridge that's full of artwork, pictures of loved ones, and notes is a beautiful sight! It just gives me a nice, homey "we live here" kind of feeling. This project is one with literally endless possibilities. If you can draw it, you can turn it into a magnet. These would also be great locker décor for those in junior high and high school.

SUPPLIES:

- Adhesive magnet paper
- White card stock
- Permanent markers
- Rubber scraper
- Scissors

1

STEP TWO
Peel the backing off of
the magnet paper.

STEP THREE
Apply the white cardstock,
using a rubber scraper to
smooth it on (the oils in
your skin can smear your
artwork).

④

STEP FOUR

Carefully cut out each magnet.

TIP!

Try this project using white sticker paper, and make your own stickers!

LOVE &

oh hello!

Don't FORGET ↓

eggs
milk
yogurt
soap
dog food

STEP FIVE
Stick them on your fridge and
enjoy your creativity!

DIY PENCIL BOXES

When you love art and creating, you'll most likely also love buying a ton of pencils, pens, and markers. And you'll need somewhere to store them all! I love to display mine on my desk in coffee mugs or these DIY pencil boxes so I can easily see all my supplies and color options!

Visit your local office supply store to find an assortment of pencil boxes. Gel pens work really well on the kraft paper style boxes due to the matte finish. Permanent markers work best on the pencil boxes that are glossier.

SUPPLIES:

- Paper-covered pencil boxes
- Assorted pens & markers

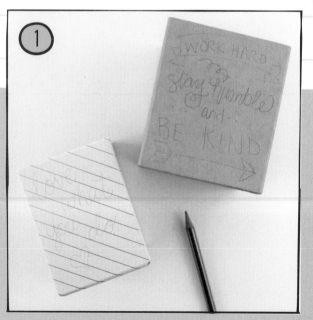

STEP ONE

Pick a phrase that inspires you. Use a pencil to sketch it on. For the kraft paper pencil box, I traced over my sketch with bright colors of gel pens and then added fun little doodles. For the pink striped pencil box, I went for a more traditional look, using a black permanent marker.

TIP!

These make an awesome gift for a teacher. Create one and fill it with pretty pens or markers. Your teachers are sure to love these!

STEP TWO

Let your boxes sit for at least 15 minutes to dry. You don't want them to smear when you erase out your pencil lines! Once dry, erase any visible pencil lines. Fill with art supplies and enjoy!

DIY SHARPIE MUGS

DIY mugs are one of my favorite things to make! I use them on my desk to organize and display all my pencils, pens, markers, and paint brushes. I've tried using several different types of markers for creating these mugs, and oil-based paint markers seem to have the most staying power.

SUPPLIES:

- Ceramic coffee mugs
- Oil-based paint markers (such as Sharpie®)

STEP ONE

Make sure your mug is clean and dry. To use the paint marker, shake and depress the tip on a piece of scrap paper until you see paint on the marker tip. You may occasionally need to do this again as you work. Doodle on your mug! I made three versions to give you some ideas.

②

STEP TWO

If you plan to actually use your mug for drinking, you'll need to bake it to "cure" the marker. Allow the design to set for 24 to 48 hours, then place in a cold oven and bake at 350 degrees Fahrenheit for 30 minutes. Allow mug to cool completely before removing.

TIP!

These make a great handmade gift for a friend, especially when filled with a set of bright, fun markers! Hand washing is recommended for longevity.

CHALKBOARD STYLE WOOD SIGN

Chalkboards have been trendy the past few years, but they are classic if you ask me! And that means they never go out of style. This sign just looks like a chalkboard, but you could use black chalkboard paint to make it a real chalkboard! Then use the chalk pencil to change the sign to say whatever you like, as often as you like.

SUPPLIES:

- Wood sign or wood slice
- Chalk pencil
- Paint (white and black)
- Thin paintbrush
- Foam brush

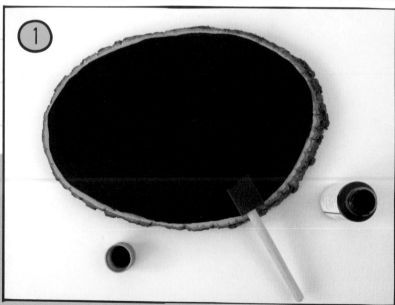

STEP ONE
Paint the wood slice or sign with black paint and a foam brush. Allow paint to dry thoroughly.

STEP TWO
Sketch out lettering on the sign with a chalk pencil.

STEP THREE

Paint over your sketch with white paint. Allow the sign to dry overnight.

TIP!

Try adding doodles into your lettering to create interest, like I've done with the arrows on this sign.

④

STEP FOUR
Use a damp soft cloth to gently
erase any leftover chalk pencil lines.

Chalkboard Style Wood Sign ♥ 61

DIY POSTCARDS

I love email, but I'm a big believer in sending traditional mail too. Not only are these DIY postcards fun and pretty, a postcard is the cheapest kind of mail you can send! I picked up a mini watercolor pad at my local craft store, and it was the perfect size for this project.

SUPPLIES:
- 4" x 6" watercolor pad
- Watercolors
- Paintbrushes
- Markers

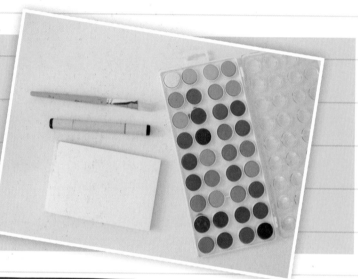

STEP ONE
Paint designs on several of your cards. For the "Hello" card, I painted a simple border with leaves and dot flowers and wrote the word "Hello" with a paintbrush. Once dry, I traced "Hello" with a fine-tip black marker.

STEP TWO

For the "Hi!" card, I painted some large polka dots, small polka dots, and trios of lines. Then I did a little splatter painting on top before adding the text.

③

STEP THREE

For the "Wish you were here…"
postcard, I used a fancier script
with a simpler watercolor design.

TIP!

Make 4 to 6 postcards and gift them as a set of handmade postcards.

STEP FOUR

After all your postcards are complete, write a little note on the back, add postage and a mailing address, and send them off to friends and family!

NATURE WORDS

Combining nature into art is one of my favorite things to do. It's a great way to get my kids involved too. We'll go on walks and look for leaves, twigs, flowers, and petals to use in photos.

Visit your local craft store to find scrapbook paper that has fun patterns. I used wood patterns, but you can use anything you like. Look for interesting textures like bricks, burlap, and glitter. You can even grab silk petals from the floral section at the craft store to use, like I did for this project.

This project is super simple and the possibilities are endless! In a well-lit area, lay out various letters and words on the scrapbook paper. Take photos of all your letters and phrases!

SUPPLIES:

- Assorted scrapbook papers
- Elements of nature (leaves, twigs, petals)
- Camera
- Basic photo editing software (I used Picasa®)

STEP ONE

The "Hi" petal art would make a great DIY notecard. To create this, just crop your photo in Picasa, print, cut, and glue to the front of a basic notecard.

STEP TWO

Combine letters to make a one-of-a-kind art print, like I did with the "LOVE" collage. To do this, I took a separate photo of each letter.

TIP!

Getting a great photo is easiest in natural light, so take your photos outside or near a window. I often use a piece of white foam core board as my background.

STEP THREE

Then I cropped each photo to a square in Picasa. Use the collage feature to group the letters into one art print!

TIP!

For a less feminine look, try using leaves instead of petals!

TIP!

Use initials or monograms to create custom wedding or anniversary gifts.

WATERCOLOR LETTERED PRINT

Watercolors are one of my very favorite mediums because they always look pretty. You don't need to be a pro to create beautifully lettered typographic watercolor art. Using watercolors to paint a custom print creates instant artwork for your room or a thoughtful handmade gift for a loved one.

Any phrase, song lyric, verse, or quote that is special to you can be transformed into one of these prints. For this project, I chose the phrase "Don't quit your daydream."

SUPPLIES:

- Notebook / Sketch pad
- Pencil
- Eraser
- Watercolor paper
- Watercolors
- Small cup of water
- Paper towel
- Small detail paintbrush
- Paint palette (a small dish will work too)

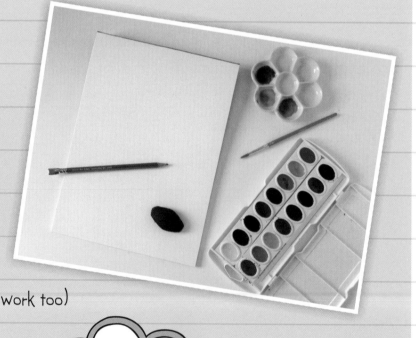

STEP ONE

Pick a phrase and sketch out some ideas on your sketch pad. Any old notebook will do. Sketching really just helps you determine a layout you like before you draw on the real print.

STEP TWO

Choose your favorite sketch and lightly draw it on a sheet of watercolor paper in pencil.

③

STEP THREE

Begin painting the phrase with your watercolors. Work slowly, but don't worry too much about "perfection." Most watercolor mistakes can be corrected by adding more water to the area and then dabbing with a small piece of paper towel or cotton swab.

TIP!

After dipping your brush in the watercolor, lightly dab on a paper towel so you don't have too much paint when you start lettering. It's much easier to add more paint than to try to fix too much!

④

STEP FOUR

Add character to your print with color, swirls, flourishes, paint splatters, dots of color…anything you like! For this print, I opted to create an ombré look by using three similar colors and changing colors for each line. Allow your print to dry thoroughly, and then gently erase any visible pencil lines.

TIP!

Trim your new print to size and glue to colored card stock to really make it pop.

PAINTED ROCK PAPERWEIGHT

Art doesn't have to be fancy or expensive, and this project is proof! Head out to your yard or visit a local park to gather some rocks for this project. Look for nice, smooth, and somewhat flat rocks that are about 3" to 4" in diameter. I found this one in my front yard. This project would make a great handmade teacher gift!

SUPPLIES:
- Rock
- Permanent marker
- Acrylic paints
- Paintbrushes

STEP ONE
Make sure your rock is clean and dry. Pick a word to write, and draw it on with a permanent marker.

STEP TWO
Paint over the word using a pointed brush and acrylic paint. If the word on your rock isn't bright enough, paint over it again until it's opaque (not able to be seen through) and visible.

STEP THREE

Now the fun part! Paint on designs. You can add lines, geometric shapes, confetti colorful dots (shown), doodles, or anything you like! Allow rock to dry thoroughly. Use as a paperweight.

TIP!

Use this method to create fun outdoor garden markers! (You might want to seal the paint for outdoor use with something like Outdoor Mod Podge® so that it stays nice and bright.)

DIY BOOKMARKS

Creating your own bookmarks with lettering and doodles is a fun project that also makes a great handmade gift idea! I usually like to start with the lettering first and then add doodles around the words. Or draw a fun border, and fill it with your chosen text.

A lot of times, the words are what inspire my doodles. For example, with the "Travel the World: Read a Book" phrase listed below, I might add a doodle of a globe, a suitcase, an airplane, or anything else travel related.

SUPPLIES:

- White card stock
- Ruler
- Pencil
- Ultra-fine-point black marker
- Colored pencils or markers
- Paper trimmer or scissors
- Colored card stock (optional)
- Paper-friendly glue (optional)

STEP ONE

Using your ruler, draw three 2½" x 6" rectangles on your sheet of white card stock in pencil.

STEP TWO

Add desired text in the center of each rectangle. Fill in the remaining white space of each bookmark with doodles.

STEP THREE

Trace over your lettering and artwork with an ultra-fine-point black marker.

STEP FOUR

Color your bookmarks with markers or colored pencils.

GET LOST IN A GOOD BOOK

5

STEP FIVE

Cut out bookmarks with paper trimmer or scissors.

inspiration IS EVERYWHERE

TAKE heart